If the World Were a Village

If the World Were a Village

Written by David J. Smith

Illustrated by Shelagh Armstrong

A & C Black • London

Acknowledgments

The effort, help and faith of many people were required for this book to be published. Jill Kneerim and Paulette Kaufmann both saw the value of it as long ago as 1992. I've had invaluable help from Barbara Bruce Williams, my agent. Val Wyatt, my editor, worked tirelessly through 14 manuscripts, never giving up hope that we would find the right combinations. And Pat Wolfe deserves special mention for everything she did. But most of all, this book is for Suzanne, my sunshine and my *bella luna*, who never stopped believing.

A note on numbers and dates

The term "billion" means different things in different parts of the world. In this book, it means one thousand million, or 1 000 000 000.

Calendars often refer to dates before the year 1 as B.C., or before Christ, and dates after the year 1 as A.D., or anno Domini, a Latin term meaning "in the year of the Lord." However, most people in the world prefer to use the terms B.C.E., or before the common era, and C.E., or of the common era. For this book about the global village, B.C.E. and C.E. have been used.

Reprinted in 2004 (twice), 2005, 2006 (updated)
Published in 2003 by
A&C Black Publishers Ltd
38 Soho Square
London W1D 3HB
www.acblack.com

Text © 2002 David J. Smith
Illustrations © 2002 Shelagh Armstrong

The right of David J. Smith to be identified as the author of this work has been asserted by him in accordance with the Copyright, Designs and Patent Act 1988.

ISBN 07136 68806
A CIP catalogue record for this book is available from the British Library.

Printed in China by WKT Company Limited

A&C Black uses paper produced with elemental chlorine-free pulp, harvested from managed sustainable forests.

Published by permission of Kids Can Press Ltd, Toronto, Ontario, Canada. All rights reserved.

Published in Canada by Kids Can Press Ltd
29 Birch Avenue
Toronto, ON M4V 1E2

Published in the U.S. by Kids Can Press Ltd
2250 Military Road
Tonawanda, NY 14150

The artwork in this book was rendered in acrylic
The text is set in Bodoni
Edited by Valerie Watt
Designed by Marie Bartholomew

Contents

Extra activities available online at
www.acblack.com/globalvillage

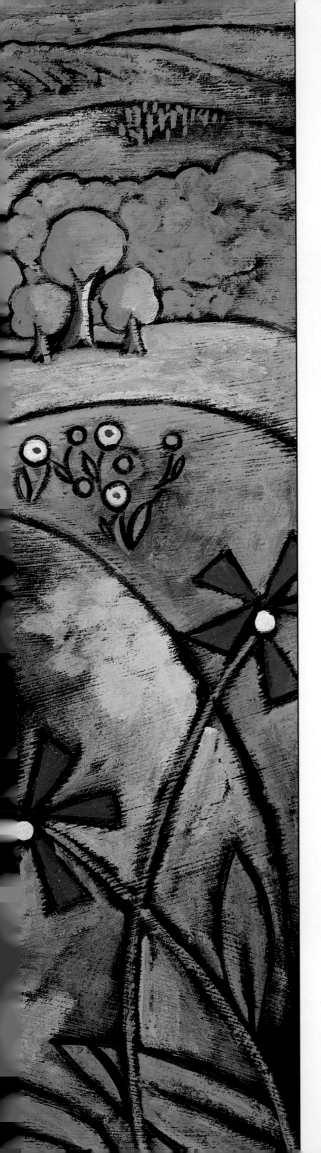

Welcome to the global village

Earth is a crowded place, and it is becoming more crowded all the time. On 1 January 2005, the world's population was 6 billion, 400 million – that's 6 400 000 000. Twenty-four countries have more than fifty million (50 000 000) people. Eleven countries each have more than one hundred million (100 000 000) people. China has one billion, three hundred million (1 300 000 000), while India has nearly one billion, one hundred million (1 100 000 000) people.

Numbers this big are hard to understand, but what if we imagined the whole population of the world as a village of just 100 people? In this imaginary village, each person would represent about 64 million (64 000 000) people from the real world.

One hundred people would fit nicely into a small village. By learning about the villagers – who they are and how they live – perhaps we can find out more about our neighbours in the real world and the problems our planet may face in the future.

Ready to enter the global village? Go down into the valley and walk through the gates. Dawn is chasing away the night shadows. The smell of wood smoke hangs in the air. A baby awakes and cries.

Come and meet the people of the global village.

Nationalities

The village stirs and comes to life, ready for a new day. Who are the people of the global village? Where do they come from?

Of the 100 people in the global village:

61 are from Asia
13 are from Africa
12 are from Europe
 8 are from South America, Central America (including Mexico) and the Caribbean
 5 are from Canada and the United States
 1 is from Oceania (an area that includes Australia, New Zealand and the islands of the south, west and central Pacific)

More than half the people in the global village come from the 10 most populated countries:

21 are from China
17 are from India
 5 are from the United States
 4 are from Indonesia
 3 are from Brazil
 3 are from Pakistan
 2 are from Bangladesh
 2 are from Russia
 2 are from Japan
 2 are from Nigeria

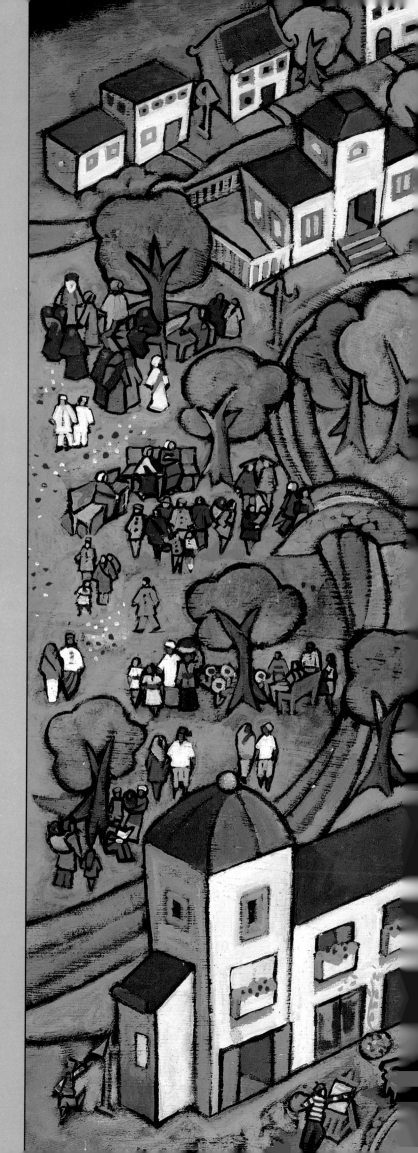

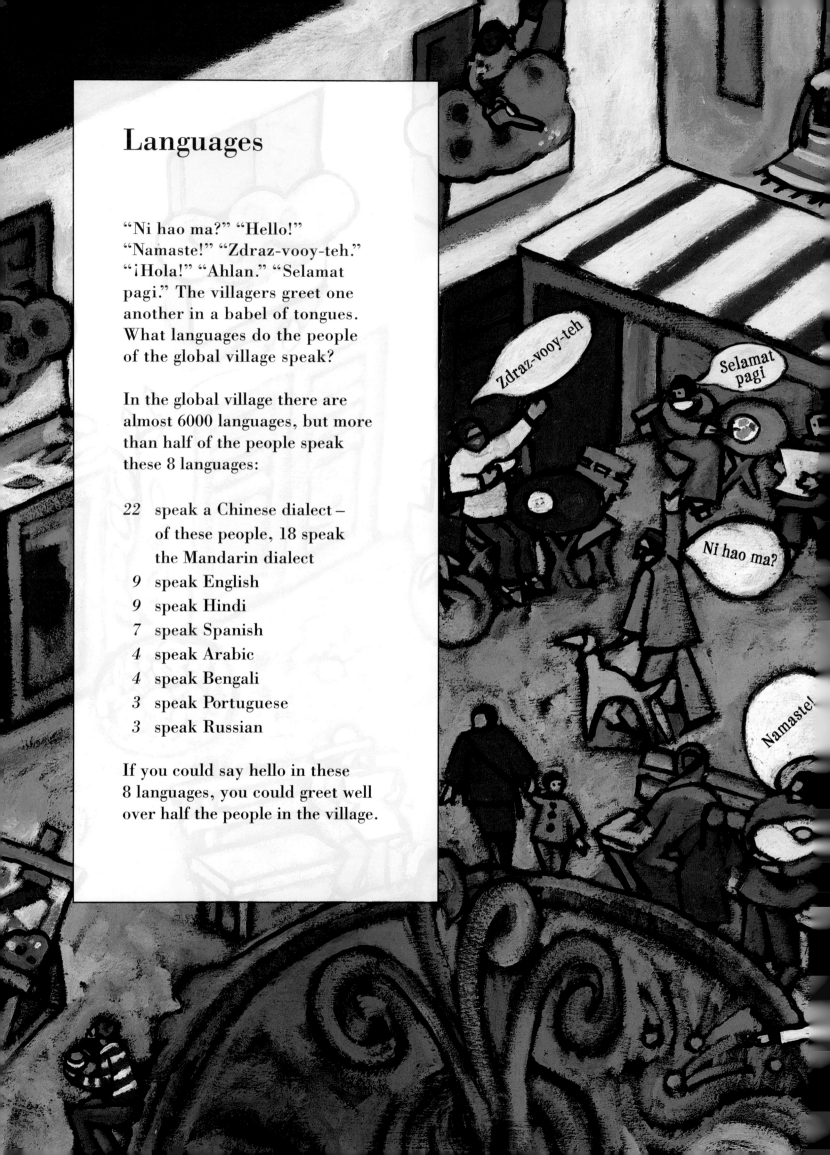

Languages

"Ni hao ma?" "Hello!" "Namaste!" "Zdraz-vooy-teh." "¡Hola!" "Ahlan." "Selamat pagi." The villagers greet one another in a babel of tongues. What languages do the people of the global village speak?

In the global village there are almost 6000 languages, but more than half of the people speak these 8 languages:

22 speak a Chinese dialect — of these people, 18 speak the Mandarin dialect

 9 speak English

 9 speak Hindi

 7 speak Spanish

 4 speak Arabic

 4 speak Bengali

 3 speak Portuguese

 3 speak Russian

If you could say hello in these 8 languages, you could greet well over half the people in the village.

Ages

A ball flies by and the children cheer. There are many children in the village. One-fifth of the villagers are 9 years of age or under. More than half are under 30. Here are the ages of the villagers:

10 are children under age 5
10 are children between 5 and 9
19 are between 10 and 19
16 are between 20 and 29
15 are between 30 and 39
11 are between 40 and 49
 9 are between 50 and 59
 6 are between 60 and 69
 3 are between 70 and 79
 1 is over 79

On average, 1 person dies and 3 babies are born every year. A baby born in the village today can expect to live to age 63.

Religions

A bell chimes in a church, a wooden gong sounds at a temple, a muezzin leads prayers from the minaret of a mosque. The villagers are called to worship.

What religions do the people of the village follow? In the village of 100 people:

32   are Christians
20   are Muslims
13   are Hindus
11   practise shamanism, animism and other folk religions
 6   are Buddhists
 2   belong to other global religions, such as the Baha'i faith, Confucianism, Shintoism, Sikhism or Jainism
 1   is Jewish
15   are non-religious

Food

The smells and sounds of the market draw you near. The tables are piled with fresh baked bread, vegetables, tofu and rice. Chickens cluck and ducks quack. In a pen not far away, a cow moos at the passing crowd.

The villagers have many animals. They help to produce food or are a source of food. There are:

- *31* sheep and goats
- *23* cows, bulls and oxen
- *15* pigs
- *3* camels
- *2* horses
- *189* chickens – yes, there are nearly twice as many chickens as people in the global village!

There is no shortage of food in the global village. If all the food were divided equally, everyone would have enough to eat. But the food isn't divided equally. So although there is enough to feed the villagers, not everyone is well fed:

- *50* people do not have a reliable source of food and are hungry some or all of the time.
- *20* other people are severely undernourished.

Only 30 people always have enough to eat.

Air and water

In most of the village, the air is healthy and the water is clean. But not all villagers are so fortunate. For some, the air and water are soured by pollution, putting them at risk of diseases. Or water may be in short supply. Instead of turning on a tap, some villagers must walk long distances to find clean water.

Fresh air and drinkable water are necessities. How many people in the village of 100 have clean air and a nearby source of clean water?

82   have access to a source of safe water either in their homes or within a short distance. The other 18 do not and must spend a large part of each day simply getting safe water. Most of the work of collecting water is done by women and girls.

60   have access to adequate sanitation – they have public or household sewage disposal – while 40 do not.

68   breathe clean air, while 32 breathe air that is unhealthy because of pollution.

Schooling and literacy

A school bell calls the young people
of the village to school. But for some
children, there is no school to go to,
or they must work instead, to help
feed their family.

How many people in the village of
100 go to school?

There are 38 school-aged villagers
(ages 5 to 24), but only 31 of them
attend school. There is 1 teacher
for these students.

Not everybody in the global village
is encouraged to learn to read,
write and think. Of the 88 people
old enough to read, 71 can read at
least a little, but 17 cannot read
at all. More males are taught to
read than females.

Money and possessions

In one part of the village, someone buys a new car. In another, a man repairs the family's bicycle, their most valued possession.

How much money do people in the global village have?

If all the money in the village were divided equally, each person would have about £3600 per year. But in the global village, money isn't divided equally.

The richest 20 people each have more than £5600 a year.

The poorest 20 people each have less than 65p a day.

The other 60 people have something in between.

The average cost of food, shelter and other necessities in the village is £2500 to £3000 per year. Many people don't have enough money to meet these basic needs.

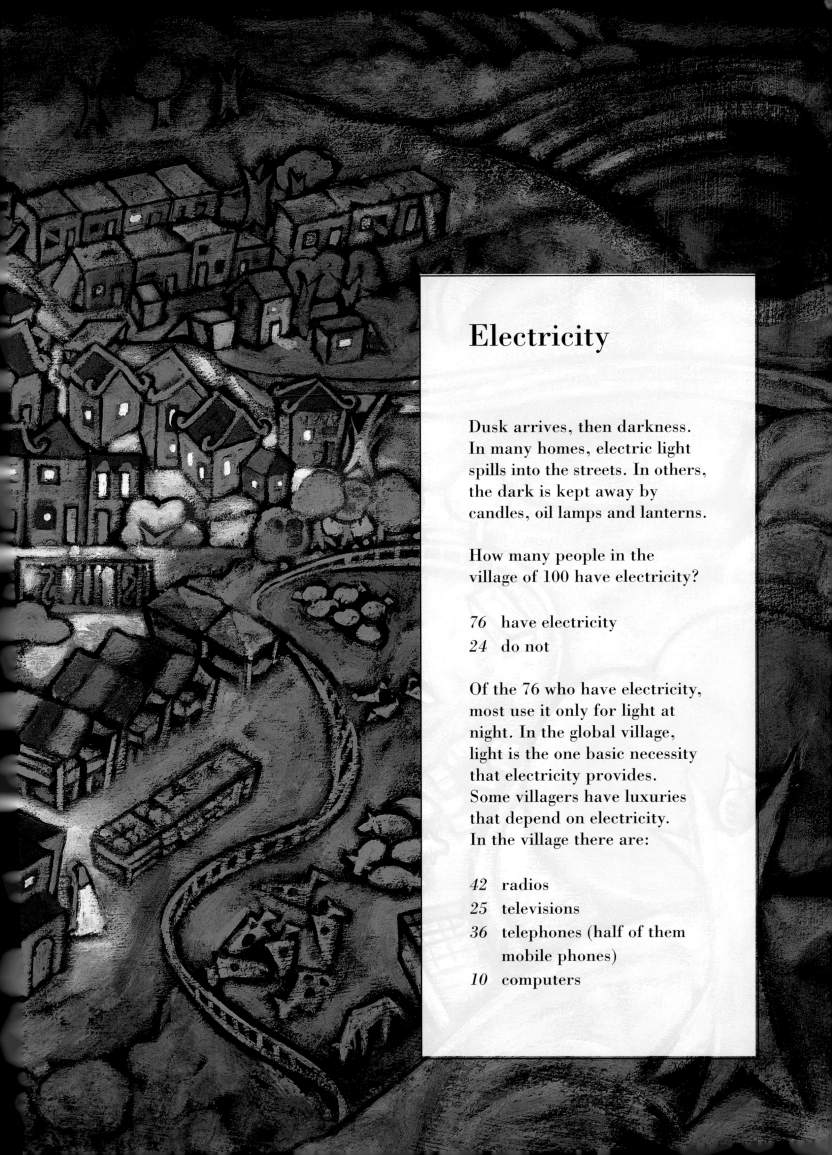

Electricity

Dusk arrives, then darkness.
In many homes, electric light
spills into the streets. In others,
the dark is kept away by
candles, oil lamps and lanterns.

How many people in the
village of 100 have electricity?

76   have electricity
24   do not

Of the 76 who have electricity,
most use it only for light at
night. In the global village,
light is the one basic necessity
that electricity provides.
Some villagers have luxuries
that depend on electricity.
In the village there are:

42   radios
25   televisions
36   telephones (half of them
     mobile phones)
10   computers

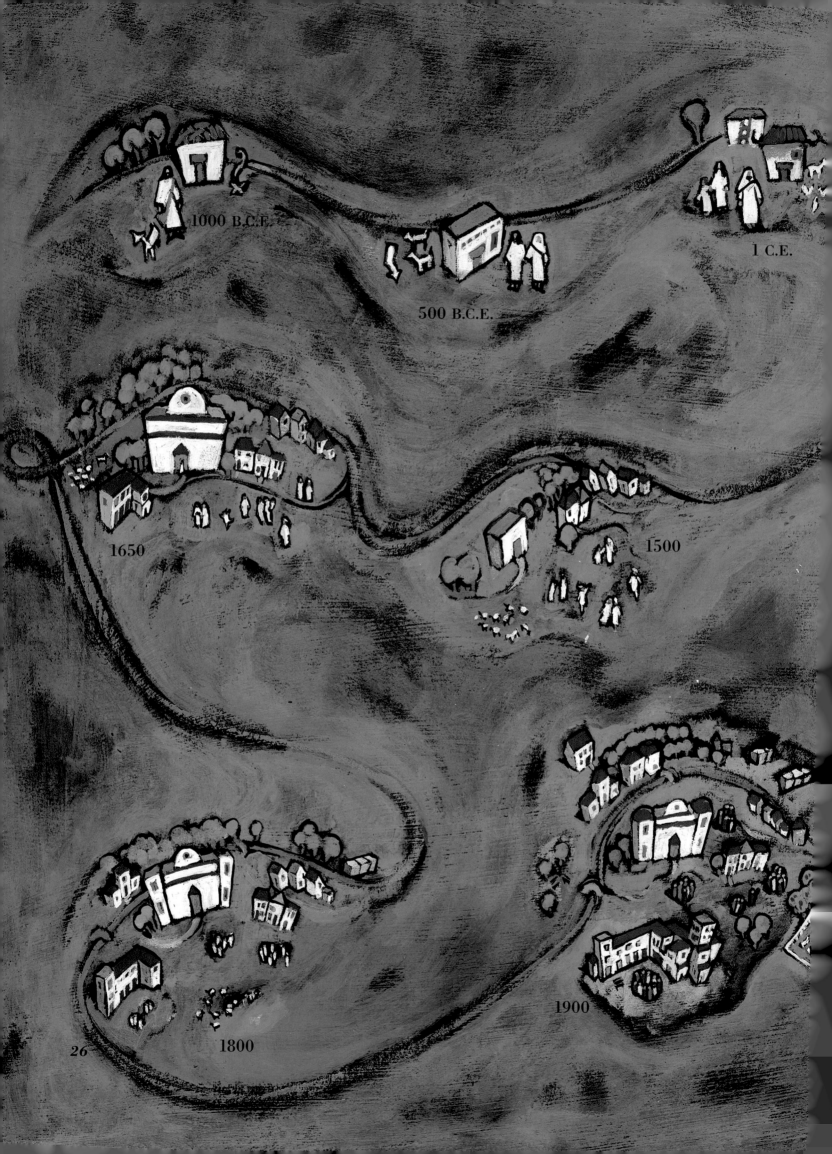

1000 B.C.E.

500 B.C.E.

1 C.E.

1650

1500

1800

1900

26

The village in the past

Today, 100 people live in the global village. How many people lived here in the past?

Over 3000 years, the population of the global village doubled 5 times, from 1 person to 2 people, to 4, to 8, to 16, to 32.

Around 1000 B.C.E., only 1 person lived in the village.

In 500 B.C.E., 2 people lived in the village.

In 1 C.E., 3 people lived in the village.

In 1000, 5 people lived in the village.

In 1500, 8 people lived in the village.

In 1650, 10 people lived in the village.

In 1800, 17 people lived in the village.

In 1900, 32 people lived in the village.

In 2002, 100 people live in the village.

The village in the future

What will our village be like in the future? How fast will it grow? How many people will it be home to?

Today, the village of 100 is growing at a rate of slightly less than 2 people a year. In fact, the growth rate is about 1.6 per cent a year. If there are 100 people in 2002, there will be almost 102 in 2003.

By the year 2100 or sooner, there will be 250 people in the village. This is an important number, because many experts think that 250 is the maximum number of people the village can sustain. Even then, there may be widespread shortages of food, shelter and other resources.

Fortunately. groups such as the United Nations and many governments and private organizations are working hard to make sure that the village of the future is a good home for all who live in it. Their goal is a global village in which food, shelter and other necessities are basic rights for all.

Teaching children about the global village

This book is about "world-mindedness," which is an attitude, an approach to life. It is the sense that our planet is actually a village, and we share this small, precious village with our neighbours. Knowing who our neighbours are, where they live and how they live, will help us live in peace.

How can parents, teachers and group leaders foster world-mindedness in children? My experience teaching and leading workshops with children all over the world has taught me a few things. Here are some guidelines and examples of activities you might want to try.

• Make sure children have a map of the world in their heads. A strong sense of world geography lays a foundation for discussions with or about people of other regions, countries and cultures.

Have a good, up-to-date world map prominently displayed on a wall. Refer to it to locate places in the news, countries where friends or relatives are travelling, areas where the books you are reading are set, and so on. Also, if possible, have at least one atlas with a good index, so that you and your children will be able to find places and explore the world more easily.

Play geography games while on car trips, at meals, before school – anytime there is a lull. For example, try What's Next?, a game in which one person names two contiguous countries, counties or states, and the other people have to work out what the next contiguous place is. So if I said, "Canada, United States," you'd say "Mexico," because if I went from Canada to the United States, the next country on my trip would be Mexico. If I said, "India, Nepal," you'd say "China"; if I said "Liberia, Ivory Coast," you'd say "Ghana."

Capital/Country is another good game. One person names a capital or a country and the other players name the missing capital or country. For example, if I said, "Lithuania," you would name the capital, Vilnius. If I said, "Astana," you'd name the country, Kazakhstan.

Or play Details, in which one person names a country and the other players give details about it. For example, for Italy, the details might be: capital is Rome; language is Italian; borders France, Switzerland, Austria and Slovenia; east is the Adriatic Sea, west is the Tyrrhenian Sea and south are the Ionian and Mediterranean Seas; entirely contained within it are the countries of San Marino and Vatican City.

Most importantly, ask questions all the time: Where is that? Where do they live? What language do they speak? What's it like there?

• Connect learning with doing. While knowledge of the world map is a vital first step, it is crucial to get children doing things with people in other countries and cultures. This can be done in person or at a distance, through regular or electronic mail, web activities and global teleconferencing.

Many websites have been constructed purely for this purpose. You'll find links to these sites through the large index and gateway sites, such as Yahoo! (http://www.yahoo.com)

If you don't have access to the worldwide web, or don't want to use it, try networking. See if you can prove "six degrees of separation": ask a child to get a letter to someone in, say, Israel by sending the letter to somebody who may know somebody in that part of the world. Is it possible to get the letter to its destination via only six people? Remember to ask the recipient to write back to explain how the letter reached him or her.

Set up a partnership or twinning arrangement between your child's school and a similar school or group in another country.

If your community is twinned with a community elsewhere in the world, get some information from your local government about the paired community and write to it.

• Help children learn to identify what they don't know. When studying the world and its people, think in terms of *possible* answers, not just *right* answers. Think also of open questions to which no answers are known. Discussion of such questions is a wonderful way to teach children how citizens think. Here are some sample questions start you off:

If there's really enough food in the world, why do some people still go hungry?

What is a country? Why are there so many new ones trying for autonomy?

Why do so many people want to live somewhere else? Where are people migrating?

What forms of government do different countries have? Why are there so many forms of government? What are the advantages and disadvantages of each? You can get specific information about forms of government from several sources. Many of these sources are listed on page 32.

What do you think could be done to help slow down the world's population growth rate?

• Foster world-minded thoughts. Look out for your neighbour. Do not break faith with anybody in the community. Service is an important part of what citizens do. Being on a team is very important.

There are no secret formulas or activities here, just one truth: if we model the behaviour, our children will follow our lead.

• Encourage passion. Do whatever is necessary to help children become passionate about their world, to discover their passions and build on and with them, and to learn from and about them. The people who are going to solve world crises 30 years from now are today's children. We'll be very, very lucky indeed if they are in a home or classroom where they acquire a passion for travel and landscape and exploration and culture and reading.

Children learn about passion from seeing it in action. What are you passionate about? How can you include children in the activities you are passionate about?

Make sure children see your love of maps and travel, your interest in news from other parts of the world and your curiosity about other people, cultures and languages. They may not follow your particular passion, but they will learn what it means to care deeply about something. If children express a strong interest in something, help them follow it up and learn more.

In a way, all the opportunities for global connections through e-mail and television make the dream of a unified world look more achievable today than it did in the past. But in other ways, the making-it-come-true part is harder than ever, especially when you consider that the global dream includes adequate food and housing, safe and affordable energy supplies and universal literacy for all, as well as the elimination of unhealthy water supplies. These goals will only be realized if we can find a way to stabilize the world's population. Six Billion Day was on 16 June 1999, and we continue to grow by 100 million people per year.

Understanding geography, the Earth and the people who live here – where, why and how – is a good starting point. However, what we need is not just facts, but a way of looking at the world that tells the story truthfully. We need to become truly world-minded and to foster that attitude in our children.

David J. Smith

A note on sources and how the calculations were made

If there are 6.4 billion people in the world, then in our village of 100, each person represents 64 million. Any time a fractional person would have appeared in our village, the number was rounded to the nearest whole number.

Many different books and resources were used to collect data on the people of our global village. The statistics were often surprising on their own. However, there was another interesting surprise – not all the sources agreed.

While there is general agreement from one source to another on most of the statistics used in this book, there is some variation from year to year and source to source. The most notable area of disagreement is in predictions for future population growth, but there are also disagreements about food supply, education and clean air and water.

Whenever possible, the most current statistics have been used; if necessary, averages or extrapolations have been made from related information.

The following sources were used for the first edition of this book. The data was adjusted in 2005 using the most recent statistics available.

Report WP/91 to WP/98, *World Population Profile*: *1991 to 1998* U.S. Census Bureau. Washington, D.C.: U.S. Government Printing Office, 1991–1998 (http://www.census.gov/ipc)

State of the World: *A Worldwatch Institute Report on Progress toward a Sustainable Society* Linda Starke, ed. New York: W.W. Norton & Co., 1994–2001 (http://www.worldwatch.org)

The Central Intelligence Agency World Factbook Washington, D.C.: Government Printing Office, 1992–2001 (http://www.odci.gov/cia/publications/factbook)

The Information Please Almanac Otto Johnson, ed. Boston: Houghton Mifflin, 1996–1998 (http://www.infoplease.com)

The New York Times Almanac John W. Wright, ed. New York: Penguin Putnam, 1997–2001

The State of the World's Children Carol Bellamy, ed. New York: United Nations Publications, 1996–2000 (http://www.unicef.org)

The Time Almanac Borgna Brunner, ed. Boston: Information Please LLC, 1999–2001

The United Nations Human Development Report United Nations Development Programme. New York: United Nations Publications, 1992–1998 (http://www.un.org)

The Universal Almanac John W. Wright, ed. New York: Andrews & McMeel, 1992–1996

The World Almanac and Book of Facts Robert Famighetti, ed. New Jersey: World Almanac Books, 1996–2001

The World Development Report World Bank. New York: Oxford University Press, 1992–2001 (http://www.worldbank.org)

World Resources: *A Report by the World Resources Institute in collaboration with the United Nations Environment Programme and the United Nations Development Programme* New York: Oxford University Press, 1992–1993 to 1998–1999 (http://www.wri.org)

Vital Signs, The Environmental Trends That Are Shaping Our Future Worldwatch Institute. Linda Starke, ed. New York: W.W. Norton & Co., 1992–1998 (http://www.worldwatch.org)

I also used many pamphlets and printouts from the UN Food and Agriculture Organization and other UN agencies, found through the UN website (http://www.un.org) and the U.S. Census Bureau website (http://www.census.gov).

The following books and atlases also provided data:

The Economist Pocket World in Figures The Economist. London: Profile Books, 1996

The Economist World Atlas The Economist. London: Profile Books, 1996

Goode's World Atlas Edward B. Espenshade, Jr., ed. Chicago: Rand McNally, 1998 (This atlas is particularly useful because it has a wonderful section of thematic maps)

The New Book of World Rankings George T. Kurian. Chicago: Fitzroy Dearborn Publishers, 1994

The Atlas of World Population History McEvedy, Colin, and Richard Jones. New York: Penguin Books, 1978

The National Geographic Atlas of the World Washington, D.C.: National Geographic Society, 1995

The National Geographic Satellite Atlas of the World Washington, D.C.: National Geographic Society, 1998